The Kite That Got Away

MW01047942

Story by Pamela Gates

Illustrations by Claire Bridge

Mom and Dad gave Ben
a beautiful kite for his birthday.
It was pink and orange,
with a red tail.
It had a long string
that went around and around
a white plastic ring.

"Let's go down to the beach
  and fly it!" said Dad.
"It's a good day for flying a kite."

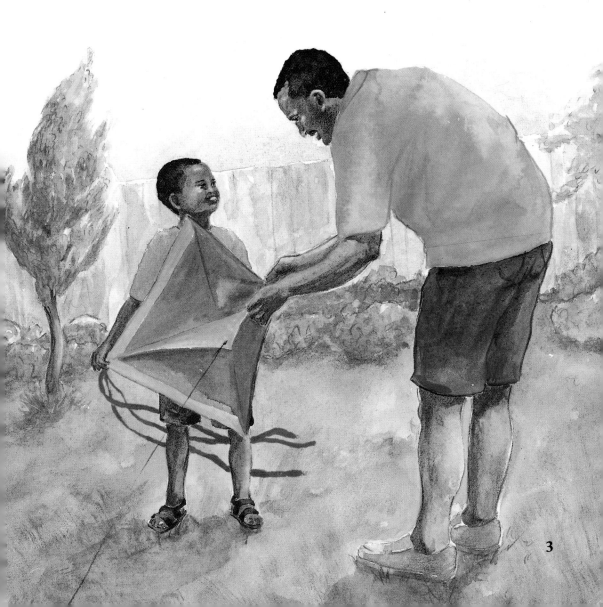

They took the kite
down to the beach.

"We will show you what to do,"
Mom said to Ben.
"Put your arm in the plastic ring.
Then the kite won't blow away
from you."

Ben put his arm in the ring
and held onto the string.

4

Dad held the kite up,
and Ben started to run
down the beach.

Then Dad let go of the kite.

The kite went way up into the air.

They all watched it.
Ben was very pleased with himself.

"That looks like fun!" said Dad.

"You can have a turn now," said Ben,
  as he pulled the kite down.
"But please be careful with it."

"I'll be careful," said Dad,
and he ran along the beach
with the kite.

Dad was looking up at the kite.
He was not watching
where he was going.

Dad tripped,
and the string slipped out
of his hand.
The kite went flying away
in the wind.

11

The kite went out over the waves.

"Oh, **no**!" cried Ben.
"My new kite is gone!
I will never get it back."

But then the kite splashed down
into the sea.

Dad ran down the beach
and right into the waves.

He got the kite just in time.

"I'm sorry I let your kite go,"
Dad said to Ben.

Ben and Mom laughed.

"You have to put your arm
in the plastic ring," said Ben.
"**Then** it won't blow away from you!"